My Mother's Scribe

Praise for *My Mother's Scribe*

'Rafiq Kathwari is a dangerous man. A poet of family history, a poet of geopolitics, he breaks down walls in his writing and leaves glittering shards whose beauties make you weep for what is and what could be. This is poetry that expects tears and earns them.

From a mother's heart-wrenching madness to a nation's lost paradise, the words confront change without flinching. Don't read this book if you are looking for anodyne reassurance. But if you want to experience the alchemy by which art draws solace from suffering, resolution from desolation, take this journey with a poet whose life has encompassed so many of our time's grim dichotomies: ethnic, religious, ideological.

Full disclosure: My objectivity about Rafiq's work is far from pure. We have known each other for some thirty years: First as fellow-toilers in writing workshops, taking apart each other's poems and suggesting "improvements" that sometimes actually made them better, then as friends and mutual admirers.

But friendship should be no bar to critical judgment. No one writes quite like Rafiq Kathwari. A master of his craft, he brings a perspective to life in the 21st century (from Kashmir to New Rochelle, from New York City to Ireland and back) that enriches our public discourse. I am grateful for our friendship; you will count yourself fortunate to encounter his unique voice in this illuminating collection of poems.'

—Gerald Jonas was a staff writer at *The New Yorker* magazine for thirty years, and a longtime contributor to the *New York Times*, writing about the sciences and the arts, and reviewing over a 1000 books of science fiction. He is the author of six books of nonfiction, and a volume of poetry.

'*My Mother's Scribe*, folds a memorable variety of genres into itself. Part memoir, part fiction, part documentary adapting found material, part dream journal, this deeply moving book traces the journeys that its protagonists, a Kashmiri family, make across the globe, from the Himalayas to the Bronx. Some of these displacements are forced, others voluntary; home is both what they lose and what they craft for themselves along the way.

Through the medium of epistolary communication—the letter, often addressed to officials or global dignitaries, is a key vehicle in these poems—Kathwari brings the lives of his protagonists into intense adjacency with the often cataclysmic events that have shaped the world since the mid-20th century. Kathwari's lifeworld is divided against itself by partition, occupation and diaspora.

Yet this lifeworld is also an accordion that brings siblings, lovers, neighbors and strangers together through acts of empathy. Loyalties are multiplied rather than divided, identities hyphenated rather than fragmented. At the heart of these poems, there remains an absent centre, celebrated in song, wept over in exile: Kashmir, a homeland reduced to a battleground, its people subjected to endemic violence.

The bond that gives this collection its title is the one between the poet and his mother—the poet wrote his mother's letters to her dictation as a child and teenager, while she retreated into a parallel reality of her own. A profound sadness inhabits these poems, yet so too do a continuity of affection, a lineage of hope. I leave you with the word *Mouje*: Mother, mother country.'

—Ranjit Hoskote is a poet, essayist and curator based in Bombay; his books of poetry include *Jonah Whale*. His translation of Lal Ded has been published as *I, Lalla: The Poems of Lal Ded* (2011).

'*My Mother's Scribe* is a very unusual set of tales and poems, actually teasing lures of tales cast as poems, personal and autobiographical, most constructed from words, feelings, experiences and letters of the poet's mother that collapse times and locations, haunted by the baleful specter of a husband who has rendered her useless and unwanted in the household by contracting a second marriage. In this microcosm of his evocation, Rafiq Kathwari brings to life an entire age, with its conflicts, discords, and betrayals before our eyes, so that the mother's travails mirror, uneasily, unsettlingly, his homeland Kashmir's, the Indian subcontinent's Partition by the British, even the situation in Palestine. A heartrending vigil, "I am a witness," writes Rafiq, "In every well in Baghdad/a rafik [a friend] is weeping . . . ," that invites reflection as much on the ills of colonialism, militarism, and religious fanaticism as on the oppressions of patriarchy, on sexual abuse, the molestation of female children in the home. A rare, exacting, illuminating collection that presents the human condition with enviable artistic economy and cleanses the heart and mind of all dross as it does so.'

—Waqas Khwaja is the Ellen Douglass Leyburn Professor of English, Agnes Scott College, Decatur, Georgia. His most recent book of poems is *Hold Your Breath* (2017).

'*My Mother's Scribe* gut-punched me. The poems are sensorial. You step into them, watching events unfold. Rafiq is a witness to the travails of his birth mother, Maryam, but through her, you also come face-to-face with the tragedies of his "motherland" Kashmir. The writing is crisp and delectable; and at times fun. Rafiq's own wit shines through to help navigate the painful burden of the maternal legacy that resides at the heart of these poems. Despite her mental challenges, humor and hope remain steadfast in Maryam. While ruing world politics and loss of homeland, Rafiq captures his mother's worldly vanities, endearing her to the reader. The apple does not fall far from the tree—this is a Kashmiri apple at that.'

—Ather Zia, Associate Professor of Political Anthropology, University of Northern Colorado Greeley, is the author of *Resisting Disappearance: Military Occupation and Women's Activism in Kashmir* (2019).

'In these exquisitely wrought "poems and tales", Rafiq Kathwari, his mother's scribe, pays homage to his mother/land, Kashmir. The poems included in this book punctuate with paradoxical lyricism, the years of Kashmir's military occupation by India, and its continuing status as a bone of contention between India and Pakistan, from the moment of its aborted plebiscite in 1949 till present times. The poems written in the mother's voice in the form of letters to different heads of state as pleas for freedom, are among the most haunting in the collection, wherein the personal and the political intertwine through tales of the Kathwari family of Kashmir, to reveal the rot at the heart of our patriarchal, uncaring world. The memory of a mother's love is the balm these poems offer to the wounds of history.'

—Fawzia Afzal-Khan is the University Distinguished Scholar and professor of English, Montclair State University and the author of *Siren Song: Understanding Pakistan through its Women Singers* (2020).

'*My Mother's Scribe* is not some mealy-mouthed requiem for a departed materfamilias but a madcap homage to someone with imagined links to the makers and shakers of her era. Kathwari does for poetry what Marquez, Kharms and Vonnegut did for prose. He lifts his readers into the extraordinary, with his own precious brand of humour and grace.'

—Gabriel Rosenstock is an Irish poet and a thaumaturgist. His most recent work, in collaboration with Kashmiri illustrator, Masood Hussain, is *Walk with Gandhi* (2019).

'Here is a threading together of loss, a muscular love story, son to mother, back-to-front and told from a world twisted out of shape, a broken place that reflects so many, and yet mirrors none. The Kashmir that Rafiq Kathwari spins together, held by poetic legacy so as to stop the essence of Kashmir from slipping through, is not a place but a prayer. "Pay attention" each stanza, free verse and piece of prose calls out. "What is madness? What is sanity?" they shout. Each line of *My Mother's Scribe* draws on poetry's miraculous capacity to reveal what the head finds so hard to hear from the heart.'

—Justine Hardy, a British author based in India who reported for *Financial Times*, is the founder of Healing Minds Foundation (formerly Healing Kashmir), a therapeutic and holistic mental health organization that since 2005 has been supporting and treating Kashmiris mentally scarred by the conflict and violence. Her most recent book is *In the Valley of Mist* (2009).

My Mother's Scribe

POEMS AND TALES

Rafiq Kathwari

Winner, The Patrick Kavanagh Poetry Award

YODA PRESS
79 Gulmohar Enclave
New Delhi 110 049
www.yodapress.co.in

Copyright © Rafiq Kathwari 2021

The moral rights of the author have been asserted
Database right YODA PRESS (maker)

All rights reserved. Enquiries concerning reproduction outside the scope of the above should be sent to YODA PRESS at the address above.

ISBN 9789382579762

Editor in charge: Tanya Singh
Typeset by Saanvi Graphics, Noida
Published by Arpita Das for YODA PRESS

تمن غائب کرنہ آئتین ہند باپتھ
تہ تہنزن منڈن باپتھ
یتیمن ہند باپتھ
تمدن أنی کرنہ آتین باپتھ
تہ تمن کاشرن باین ہند باپتھ
یہنزن قبرن نہ کُنہ چھ کہ نیب تہ نہ نشانے

For the disappeared
the half-widows
the orphans
the deliberately blinded
and for my fellow Kashmiris in unmarked graves

Scribe and his mother in an earlier era

CONTENTS

God in Tailcoats Makes a House Call	1
Mother Writes to President Eisenhower	2
The American Vice Consul Responds	4
Sunday Bath in the Cube	5
What Happened to a World	8
Birds of Paradise	9
Mother Writes to the Turkish Ambassador in Karachi	10
Jewel House Ghazal	12
Yeti Yanks the Crazy Quilt	13
Two Proposals 60 Years Apart	14
I Go Back to June 1939 When My Parents Wed	17
Mother Writes to Indira Gandhi	19
Indira Gandhi Responds	21
Old Forms Will Not Be Entertained	22

Hallucinations	23
Mother Leans against the Island	27
A Resurrection	30
Lost in Translation	32
Mother Writes to Her Husband's New Wife	33
The New Wife Responds	35
Mother Has the Last Word	38
I Translate Mother's Dream for Harry the Shrink	40
Dr. Qureshi Dares My Mother	42
I Hallucinate a Bomb Blast in Baggage Claim	44
Kismet	46
Last Night I Dreamt I Was in Kashmir Again	48
Capitals: A Game Farouk Plays to Keep Mother's Mind Active	50
Driving Lolita in the World's Most Militarized Zone	53
Motherboard	56
On Receiving Father at JFK after His Long Flight from Kashmir	57
Israeli Patrols Kill 90 Dogs in Arab Town	58

A Son Writes to His Mother	59
Poem without a Title	60
After Seeing Caryl Churchill's Seven Jewish Children	63
Cravings	64
Pages from My Father's Diary	65
When I Ask	68
Veracity	69
Karl Marx Ignites the Millennials	70
Whirling	71
A Mother's Eulogy for Her Son	73
Mother Writes to Admiral of the Fleet Louis Francis Albert Victor Nicholas Mountbatten, 1st Earl Mountbatten of Burma (born Prince Louis of Battenberg), Last Viceroy of India, Cuckolded by Nehru, Assassinated by the IRA	74
My Dinner with Agha Ashraf Ali	77
The Day I Was My Sister's Chaperone	78
For My Nephew Omar on His Engagement to Nadia	79
Mother Writes to the Father of her Children, her Long-Deceased Husband	81
Found in Translation	84

My Mother's Scribe	85
Where Are the Snows of Yesteryear?	86
Obit	89
Glossary	93
Gratitude/Shukriya	103
First Publication Credits	109
About the Poet	113

My Mother's Scribe

Rafiq Kathwari

God in Tailcoats Makes a House Call

Moonbeams back into my throat,
she pleads with a god in tailcoats.

An angel straps her ankles
pads her temples

shoves a rag in her mouth
pins her fleshy arms

kisses her eyes closed.
God in tailcoat

flicks on his volt box.
Bulbs flicker. She sizzles.

Cold full moon of Kashmir
discovers her attic room

where a boy,
birthmark on forehead,

tiptoes to his mother's bed.
She calmly asks me my name.

Rafiq Kathwari

Mother Writes to President Eisenhower

6 August 1956

Dear Mr. President,

I'm your shadow under the Kashmir sky.
My 7- and 9-year-old boy and girl
are over there across the Cease Fire Line
and my younger four are with me
over here on this side of Partition.

Children who grow up apart don't know
how to say goodbye.
Gods of wrath have flung me
into an unloved city where flowers are dusty,
and branches are weeping.

Even birds have stopped singing.
My home feels empty. Why
can the blessed nuns at Jesus & Mary
Convent, Murree readily cross the Line
to teach at the Presentation Convent,

Srinagar, and my children can't? Gods
of wrath are killing my memory.
A mother without memory has no history.
I shield myself with silence.
A voice speaks inside my heart. Often,

I wish to make myself wings, and fly.
I have run out of tears, Mr. President.
You are the sky and the earth. Please
tear down all walls dividing people,
not just in Kashmir but wherever

children become barricades. Please
show the world our resolve
by printing this in *The New York Times*.
Good luck in your bid for re-election.
I'll pray for your victory. Sincerely,

Mrs. Maryam Jan,
Muzaffarabad,
Pakistan-administered Kashmir.

Rafiq Kathwari

The American Vice Consul Responds—(*excerpted*)
20 August 1956

Dear Mrs. Jan,
I have been asked to reply for the President.
The United States Government is always glad
to hear various views concerning
the very important Kashmir question,
and we found your letter really interesting.

You will understand, I am sure, newspapers
in the United States are not controlled
by the government, and we are therefore
unable to have your letter published. You
may be assured, however, the United States

will continue to support a just solution
of the Kashmir problem. Thank you again
for your letter. Very truly yours,
For the Consul General, Robert P. Smith,
Vice Consul, Lahore, West Pakistan.

Sunday Bath in the Cube

My sister latched the door:
A tube of light through the pane
shocked the cement floor.

My kid brother, Tarek, and I sat
naked near a bucket,
a canister to scoop water

Lifebuoy soap on chipped saucer,
a cylindrical container poised on bricks,
a tap crudely soldered to its hem.

Under the container,
nuggets glowed on a charcoal burner
heating up the water.

Let's be clear about this: No
shower, no tub, no sink, no mirror,
only a hole in the floor

for draining waste bath water out to a gully.
To be fair to bathrooms he had known,
Father had named it The Cube.

Dizzy and nauseous, heart faster,
beads of sweat on bony chest,
the more I breathed, the more I gasped,

wondering what was taking my sister
so long to scoop water from the bucket
and shower it on my head.

She dragged herself to the door
on tip-toe to reach the latch, fell back,
slowly rose, her fingers clawing the pane.

My kid brother collapsed
on the floor, his mouth an O.
Are we playing dead?

Charcoal, the Mother of All Coals,
Father later said, burns quickly
in airtight rooms, releases deadly gas.

You can't see, smell, or taste it.
Inhaled, it displaces oxygen
we breathe to stay alive.

I remember only blurs: Glass
shattering, treetops waving, sirens,
a cold mask on my face: Breathing.

Farouk, older brother, waiting
his turn to bathe, sat on a small
crate outside The Cube, reading

Superman, wondered
why no waste water flowed
out to the open gully

in the courtyard. He bolts upstairs
to tell Father, who runs down
without touching the handrail,

breaks the pane, unlatches the door,
drags us all out, and sends Farouk
on his Hero bike to summon Red Cross.

My sister gradually grew
protective of me and my kid brother
who stopped sucking his thumb, after all.

Praised for his presence of mind,
Farouk promised but never gave me his comics
and never lets us forget his heroics.

Seeing her three angels in mortal poses,
Mother rips her blouse,
Pummels her bosom. *There is no god*

but God, no god but God, no god.
The next day, my parents sacrifice
a lamb, give meat to other refugees

camped in Muzaffarabad
near the ceasefire line,
after the first war over Kashmir.

Rafiq Kathwari

What Happened to a World

I open my jaw to maa
purse my lips to moo
fleece white as snow on K2

Bathe my lamb Maamoo
in an oval tin tub
under a grand oak

Eid al-Adha
Day of Sacrifice
Father ropes Maamoo's legs

feeds him sugar
'to sweeten the blow'
Mother pulls at her hair

pleading with Father
Knife at Maamoo's throat
in the name of Allah

Bismillah
blood crescent
soaking grass

Maamoo's head at my feet
eyes reflecting light
of dead stars

Birds of Paradise

Two Birds of Paradise
on the Tree of Life
dazzle the wall above
his king-size bed

He names the female bird
after my cousin Sofia
heartless tease at fourteen
I too fancy her

feigning sleep in his bedroom
on a corner chaise
my fingers tremble
above combed fringes

Perched on a branch
the male yearns for flight
his one-eyed gaze fixed
upon Grandfather's hand

fondling Sofia on the bed
The female flutters in midair
plumes fanning out
brilliant madder dyes

Rafiq Kathwari

Mother Writes to the Turkish Ambassador in Karachi

17 April 1958

Your Excellency,
thank you for the portrait
of Mustafa Kemal Ataturk
who yanked the women of Turkey
kicking and screaming
into the 20th century.

Please accept this modest shawl I promised.
Every stitch hand-embroidered
by the blessed women artisans of Kashmir
who have spilled their sadness
with threads and barbed wire,
weaving the wrath of history.

An iron necklace frames the square shawl.
Four doves with broken wings sit in corners.
Himalaya gallops the wind.
A river rises to discover clouds.
A moon in the center grins
back at a helmeted head
shooting at her, as you will see.

The blessed women artisans
of Kashmir convey best wishes
to the brave daughters of Turkey.

I hope Ankara undoubtedly supports
our right to self-determination. We

have been fighting long for freedom.
We thank you and your country
for the goodwill you have shown.

Yours faithfully, Mrs. Maryam Jan,
Katrina Bungalow, Pindi Point,
Murree, West Pakistan.

Rafiq Kathwari

Jewel House Ghazal

In Kashmir, half-asleep, Mother listens to the rain.
In Manhattan, I feel her presence in the rain.

A rooster precedes the Call to Prayer at Dawn:
God is a namedropper: All names at once in the rain.

Forsythias shrivel in a glass vase on her nightstand.
On my windowsills, wilted petals, a petulance of the rain.

She must wonder when I will put on the kettle.
Butter the toast, observe silence in the rain.

She veils her hair to offer a prayer across the oceans.
Water on my hands becomes a reverence of the rain.

At Jewel House in Srinagar, Mother reshapes my ghazal.
No enjambments, she says. Wow! Excellence in the rain.

Rafik, I hear her call out a name above the city din.
The kettle whistles: Mother's scent in the rain.

Yeti Yanks the Crazy Quilt

'You are a prophet. You are.'
She mimics cock-a doodle-do

A Shiva of the Skies
booms Himalaya. She dashes

to a window shrieking,
'Firewood up yours,'

her fists blossoming. Returns
to bed where her yeti

yanks the crazy quilt over
her head like a tea cozy.

Tense on my soft mattress,
I block my ears and watch

an astounded rooster beating
his wings against a pane.

Rafiq Kathwari

Two Proposals 60 Years Apart

1938

She circles the room,
two men cross-legged

on woven flowers,
her kohl-lined eyes downcast

to her shining sandals
at the fringes

the fluted foot
of a samovar,

henna petals on her toes.
Look, my child has no flaws,

no need to give ear to rumors,
her father tells the intended

father-in-law
who's in Srinagar for the viewing

months before the wedding.
Intended father-in-law—

an expert d'objets d'art
shakes her father's hand, deal-sealed—

gives her filigreed silver
wedged heels with pointed tips

too big for the girl she was,
bunions not yet formed.

1998

Again I ease her palm into mine
We stroll the beach

Frangipani petals
Rushlight

Inks of her sarong
My bruised jeans

Gods on horses
Spark the horizon

It's a sign, I know
What sign? she asks

Rafiq Kathwari

Marry me!
Ask me again—

She jolts me
And yet once more

Her gritty palm is mine
Bending a knee I ask

Will every flower from
Kenya to Kashmir bloom?

I Go Back to June 1939 When My Parents Wed

As arranged, they meet the first time.
He law student, she child bride.

She wears red: For rancor?
Head bowed, veiled little stars

in gold thread, waits on the bed
like an arrow drawn on a bow.

Henna-touched hands, a mirror poised
on lap: A girl staring back.

If he sits beside her,
She'll see him glance at her image.

In the courtyard, children sing,
'Petals fall from almond trees.'

The singing could continue until
he displays a blood-stained sheet.

Footfalls on stairs, whispers,
robes rustling, attar of roses.

His hand on her chin, her heart leaping.
He kisses her eyes closed.

Stop. Sever the bond, I want to scream.
He'll play possum, make you prey.

The mirror slips from her fingers,
bangles clash on fleshy arms.

Mother Writes to Indira Gandhi

The Hon'ble Mrs. Indira Gandhi,
Prime Minister, New Delhi

7 July 1975

Dear Madam,

How are you?
What's with this Emergency?
India's star is fading
while you're sexing guru
Brahmachari.

A pilot *bucklemeups*
in his *sexjet*.
Pompous rogue increased wireless
whispering, murmuring
shor shanti shor shanti
Indira Ji, please heed my plea:
Empty the sky. Show your ire.
Command him at once ceasefire.

A woman's mind is no man's land.
I hang my *vaginarags*
out on a string—pale buntings
fluttering Kashmir's fragrant breeze.

Rafiq Kathwari

My husband remarried.
She burps, yawns, farts, is fertile
and thick as two planks.
Will she leave him alone at dawn
to write his diary?

Her two readymade children
call me, Big Mom, *Badi Ammi*.
My husband says new wife
will be my caregiver.

It's tearing me apart, Madam,
and I'm again losing my mind.
Faithfully, Mrs. Maryam Jan,
River View, The Bund, Srinagar.

Indira Gandhi Responds—(*Imagined*)

New Delhi
30 July 1975

Dear Maryam Jan,
Many people have no clue about the fine line
between madam and madness.

There is an insurgency in my own emergency
with the Brahmachari.

People want rights without responsibilities.
A dose of self-enlightened rule should give India pause.

Remember, hearts are not broken. They're bruised.
Wish I was under the Kashmir sky.
Affectionately, Indira.

Old Forms Will Not Be Entertained

(A sign at the India Consulate, New York)

Old chants to the Ganges shall not be entertained
Dead cows float in holy water unrestrained

Family roots shall be ascertained
Nationality of mother should reign

Old friends shall not be entertained
I pledge allegiance to the nuevo-famed

Object of Journey shall be explained
To probe etymology of Kashmir-curfewed

Old profession shall not be entertained
Shall I reincarnate as Poet-un-Chained?

An old form (in triplicate) shall be obtained
drained, birdbrained, and scatterbrained

Enemy passports will be stamped Foreordained
Will heart-rending appeals ever be sustained?

Alternative gods shall be deported
Against the ruins of a world what is regained?

Hallucinations

After my father died, I flew to Kashmir to bring Mother to New York. Here's what she said to me when we met in her small room.

The servants never listen to me
    only when the new wife nods
they run around like rats
    to fetch the thermos

There's poison in the spring water

Chanel!
A present from my son Farouk
    in America—the wind
carried my message
    after all

Thieves
    under my bed
I want latches on my door
    and a mirror

The old one shattered
    when the nail gave way
I hang
    my shawl on the wall

Rafiq Kathwari

Dried roses
        upside down
my room
        not swept for six days

no water
to soak clothes
my daughter will clean
        when she visits

The door is bolted
        from outside
If the house catches fire who'll
        open it?

Will I burn alive?
        The servants' outhouse
turns my stomach
        a pane is broken I'll spray Chanel!

My grandson from his
        grave has come here on a visit
He's with his great-grandfather
        they both received transfusions

My husband says
        I don't need a doctor
but that doesn't keep his new wife
        from going to the Combined Hospital

I. Am. Still. The. Head. Of. This. Household.

O Wind
        tell my son in America
the dollars he sends
        the new wife misspends

Tell him I need a car
        to buy roses
at Shalimar
        My husband has lost interest

in roses
        For years he's been saying
Maryam is mad mad
        Is there anything wrong with me?

My sky is vaster than my mind
        my son builds homes for me
in America
        Sea views and rolling hills

where the Maharaja of Kashmir
        exhales—
no water
        I have no water

Rafiq Kathwari

The servant washing dishes
        keeps it from reaching me
everyone has cancer
        including the midwives

O North wind
        what's taking my grandson so long?
dead mosquitoes
        in my denture bowl

Mother Leans against the Island

in
the
nanosecond
kitchen
at
Farouk's
home,
New
Rochelle.
Miracle
Icemakers
create
half-
moons.
She
cheerily
spins
Lazy-
Susan.
Clicks
fire
fountains
on
off.
'Atomic
food
makes
stomachs

ache,'
startles
the
microwave.
'I
remember,'
she
says,
'squatting
in
front
of
a
clay
oven,
blowing
my
lungs
to
light
a
fire.
My
smoke-
singed
eyes,
your
father's

scorn—'
She pulls out an empty tray from the oven, 'For 50 years I created a home only to see the new wife inherit it.'

Rafiq Kathwari

A Resurrection

My mother tells this story
about her childhood in Kashmir
years before she married my father.

'I remember our horse Burak,
hoofs scuffing snow, nostrils fuming,
hitched to an open cart. Relatives,

showering rice and rose petals
on Mohammed's shrouded body—
the son my father always wanted

to whom I was betrothed—
wailed not for a soul departed
but sang of a bride waiting

for an intended groom
who succumbed
to the Mother of All Chills.'

Four score and three years later
Mother rises from the bright
Ethan Allen tight back couch

in New Rochelle
to do what now she does best
—merging time past and time present—

whispers across Long Island Sound,
'Mohammed,
have they given you a transfusion?'

Rafiq Kathwari

Lost in Translation

I have a radio in my head
and I'm forever listening

to whispers, always whispers,
Mother tells Harry the Shrink,

who puts a rubber band on her arm
and flicks it. Did that turn

off the radio? he asks.
She winces, removes the band,

You've made this into child's play,
she says, swiveling her chair

to glare at me, her fifth child,
reclined on the couch

translating Kashmiri,
mother tongue.

Mother Writes to Her Husband's New Wife

7 April 2014

Dear Suraya,
my son Farouk says his home with views
of the sea belongs to me, but the glint
in his eye reminds me of the glint
in his father's eye when he used to say,
which wasn't often, I was his only

beloved wife. The rogue who hounded me
in Kashmir disrupts my dreams here as well.
The rascal defies even U.S. laws,
digging deeper to find more than gold.
Don't treat me like a child, I tell Giselle,

maid from Haiti, who's her own museum,
as she ties a bib around my neck. How
long shall I bear this circus? My son pledged
to fly me back to Kashmir, but I know
he's only teasing. 'Stay, now you are here,'

he says, his eyebrows leap like a vine.
'Who's going to care for you there in winter?
No power. No heat. No water. Dal Lake
ice. Army sharmy everywhere.' Yet, I yearn
to see almond trees bloom, my grandchildren.

Rafiq Kathwari

I hope you've repainted my room
in the attic, installed western style commode,
for I'm still the head of my home. All my
love all around as always, Fondly,
Maryam, New Rochelle, New York.

The New Wife Responds

10 April 2015

Dear Maryam Jan,
your son is a rock.
I'm heartbroken
to tell you
the family house
full of memories
collapsed
in Flood of the Century
past September.
A lake that had formed
over time from
the drip, drip, drip
of a large glacier broke
its bank and the raging
waterfall overwhelmed
the Jhelum
which flooded Srinagar,
turning it into a lake
it once was.

We're building
a new cottage
with bricks and timber
salvaged from remains

of the ancestral house.
That'll be your new home.
In fact, we have named it
Maryam.
We shall share my king size bed,
modern bathroom fixtures
for your comfort, a non-
nattering nanny from Nepal,
perhaps as good as
your Haitian maid.

Fresh, crimson roses
from the Shalimar will bloom
on your nightstand
for I know how you love
bright colors and delicate scents.
I shall serve you,
as I did for a generation,
to the extent I can
with what I have,
best I know how.

Your grandchildren,
great grandchildren,
and now—congratulations!
You've one great-great grandson
as well—all will at once

shower you with almond
blossoms when you return
to your new home.

All our love from all to all.
Fondly, Suraya,
Raj Bagh, Behind Convent School,
Srinagar, Kashmir (India).

Rafiq Kathwari

Mother Has the Last Word

Fire log in cunt,
a pious father yells
at his daughter—

(Now this sounds authentic.
but would a Kashmiri father
use this word?

Few would in the West.
Few do in the East.
But this isn't fiction.)

—who tells him
an egg she swallowed has grown
into a chick inside her belly.

Certain his only child is possessed.
He buys a perky hen to entice
the chick and purge it.

Hen flutters in his hands
as he chases his daughter
barefoot around their backyard

a day after snow.
The daughter hops
like 'the snow hare

that lunges deep into the throat
of a glacier to outrun the elk'
and eludes the fuming father.

Three score and three years later,
she plumbs a memory,
summons all her frail strength

to yell, Fire log in prick,
back at her long-deceased father,
who she insists in a shrill voice

is alive at her childhood home
in Kashmir. At Farouk's home
in New Rochelle,

in my usual heartless way
I administer Ativan and Zyprexa
to chill Mother's mind.

Rafiq Kathwari

I Translate Mother's Dream for Harry the Shrink

Naked,
except for my nikab,

roped to a round pillar
on a sand dune

the sun's anvil,
my feet dancing.

Turbaned Bedouin,
henna-dyed beard,

Champion Lovemaker,
peace be upon Him,

raked His fingers at me.
Quicksand rose to my thighs.

My heart sank.
I awoke.

>   Harry the Shrink turns towards me
>   and says, repressed sexual fantasy,
>
>   need for intimacy.
>   Nakedness: Vulnerability;

nikab veiling her face
below the eyes: Anonymity.

Bondage suggests either
a desire to be submissive, or

a yearning to be free.
Sinking into quicksand:

Reversion into the subconscious.
Guilt about her desires

drives her to religion—
the Champion Lovemaker—

to rekindle her,
make her feel better.

What is he saying? Mother asks.
It's my dream, after all.

I resort to diplomacy. Mother,
doctor sahib says I should help you

write down or tape-record your dreams.
Mother nods. Harry grins. I shrug.

Rafiq Kathwari

Dr. Qureshi Dares My Mother

'Maryam Jan,' he says, 'you must be proud
of your son Farouk, his wealth—praise Allah—
how he has made himself great in America.'

The doctor's white hair is unruly like mine,
his bifocals tipsy, elbows resting
on the mahogany table hand-crafted

in Mexico exclusively for Ethan Allen,
classic Yankee firm Farouk reinvented
over the past 30 years over and over again

to help those who need help to make their homes
beautiful. My brother sits as usual at the head, his hair
slicked back, eyebrows arched at the dare.

Waitaminute, how unfair of the doctor
who goads my *Ammi* to choose favorites between
two sons, her *betas*, a Chairman of the Board

bankroller of *Ammi's* pricey healthcare,
and a dim bulb in the six-light trumpet
chandelier bouncing off the buffed grain.

Dear doctor, faithful friend, first Pakistani champ
of the Scarsdale Bridge Club—*mashallah*—keep on
injecting *Ammi* with B12, her weekly fix, hear

her heart beat, hold her gnarled hands
as she begs you to use your wealth of healing
savvy, even declare Martial Law to please stop

voices, only voices always in her head,
but don't provoke her as she sits up on
a Chippendale, sips saffron-infused Kashmiri

kahva from a china cup, a gold-rimmed hem
dupatta slips to her shoulders,
more geography than physiology on her face,

'Doctor sahib,' she says, meeting his gaze
across the wide expanse of burnished veneer,
'I'm proud of all my children.' Soaring

above the shore of Long Island Sound
I'm as far from New Rochelle
as America is from a crescent moon.

Rafiq Kathwari

I Hallucinate a Bomb Blast in Baggage Claim

I grow wings
sprinting the tarmac

single file khakis
blurred flush of poppies

My legs collapse
I roar over tips

of poplars in Srinagar
shadow the Jhelum

upstream to Verinag
fresh water spring

where Mother
tears open

with bare hands
a pomegranate

Rubies she says
my dowry

pinched by in-laws
Her dupatta ripples

she's airborne
reclined on the veil

Mohammedan angels
soar the Kush

Pallor of twilight
over the Pacific

In the Bronx
a billboard

GILDED CAGE FOR THE DERANGED

rises to greet me
I search for Mother

Waitaminute, a brown Buddha says
Why aren't you already where you're going?

Rafiq Kathwari

Kismet

This can't be me, Mother says,
leaning forward in a wheelchair.
Some other shriveled woman,

with parched skin, frayed hair.
Not me. I'm only 30. Mother
hands back my smartphone

with which I clicked her photo
during a commercial break,
watching *Kismet*,

Hollywood film made in the '50s
when Mother was in fact 30
with six children

in Kashmir.
Her skin then was smooth;
hibiscus bloomed in her hair.

Now, 64 years later
at Hebrew Home for the Aged,
The Bronx

in Mother's sparse room,
a harem girl on T.V., decked out
in baubles, bangles, and beads,

starts revolving
in the Caliph's courtyard
in Old Baghdad,

pantaloons blooming,
turban glittering:
I grit my teeth, glaring

at a fantasy Orient, thinking
of Iraq in ruins today.
Mother is transfixed

as the harem girl twirls
to stage front where her flawless
face fills the full screen.

Suddenly, Mother sighs.
What's wrong, I ask gently,
massaging her stiff fingers

with Aspercreme. Mother nods
at the T.V., whispers,
I want my skin like hers.

Rafiq Kathwari

Last Night I Dreamt I Was in Kashmir Again

'May our chinar tree last a thousand years,'
Grandfather said, clenching a cigar.
'Chi means What, Nar: Fire: What Fire!'

Rustling boughs reigned above the tin roof
of our home where I was born a Scorpio
at midnight. In autumn each leaf burst into

a flower. We gathered the remains of dyes
to create fuel for winter, sprinkling water
on burning leaves, palms brushed ashes

together, packing cinders in a clay pot
intertwined in bright wicker, his kangri.
'A symbol of our culture,' he said,

cloaking it between his knees under
a loose mantle, his phiran, three yards
of brown houndstooth made by Salama,

beloved tailor at Polo View, solely
for Grandfather who said the embers
warmed his bones. 'We are all bones

under the houndstooth,' my father said.
He was sun-withered, pouring morning tea
from a samovar alone beside an amputated

trunk. *What's Father doing in Kashmir,*
have they annulled the Partition?
But he still parts his hair in the center.

A Himalayan glacier ruptured its bank.
The valley was again a lake it used to be.
I was a shikara I was rowing. I was

crewel curtains adorning the shikara I was
moments ago. I was a signal tower collapsed.
Barrenness had become a thousand things.

Rafiq Kathwari

Capitals: A Game Farouk Plays to Keep Mother's Mind Active

Moscow!
Mother says
when Farouk asks,

Capital of Russia?
Japan? he asks

Tokyo! she says,
gazing at the fireball

of sunset mirrored in a pane
across the courtyard.

You were born
a week after Nagasaki,

she says to Farouk
who arches his eyebrows,

gently rubs her gnarled fingers
but keeps on playing.

Germany? he asks.
Munich! she says.

No. Berlin, he says—
and you, standing at the footboard,

think to what purpose
reprising history

of human madness
in the 20th century?

So many hardy women—here
Hebrew Home the Bronx

lived through the horror
of nuking humans

horror of Partitions
of Holocausts

of a Cold War in Europe
the horror of hot wars in Asia—

so many tough women like Mother,
paragraphs of pyrrhic pride

writ on their worn faces,
declining on soft beds—

yes, declining, not reclining—
who now play along

with prosperous sons
in posh pavilions

named for patrons
who would annex

planets beyond the moon
if they could.

Capital of Israel? Farouk asks.
A trick question, she says
chuckling. Falasteen.

Driving Lolita in the World's Most Militarized Zone

A boy, I hid in grandpa's study.
An art dealer he loved books
with gilded edges, Aristotle to Zola
stuck together in the humidity.

I snuck Lo out to his black Chevy,
rifled for the dirty bits
(should have looked harder I guess),
took her for a spin,

teen tunes swirling in my head,
I Want to Hold Your Hand,
beamed us forward to the future —
a crackdown in downtown,

mothers hid their first-born sons.
'We fear forces'll take our boys away.'
A soldier speckled pellets on the face
of a nymphet, light of her mother's eye.

'Nothing can be seen,' the nymphet said,
'as far as the eye can see.'
Counter insurgents wrapped petrol-
soaked rags around a boy's penis,

lit a match. 'Not tortured anyone
needlessly,' they said as the Zabarvan,

white turbans on peaks,
amplified the boy's shrieks.

Full moon of Kashmir
hid her face in sullied Dal lake.
A *shikarawallah* calmed the swells
with a heart-shaped oar.

Butterflies fluttered at Pari Mahal
Memory now is muteness.
An ancient Sufi shrine gutted,
its rich latticework lost.

New architecture
showed no awe for Nature.
Half-widows wailed, clawing
at mass graves, yearning

for their disappeared.
A paisley-shaped river
sobbed through a dazed valley.
Concrete barriers fenced the Shalimar,

bullet riddled Toyotas in bazaars.
Amputated trees lost their esteem,
reams of plastic choked mountain streams.
'We are all lifeless here. Hello!

Yehthe laege nave tav taylephone.'

At Zero Bridge
lilacs by bunkers bloomed.
A nightingale sang of sorrow.

'Why are you here?'
my mother asked, sipping salt tea
at the Mental Hospital, Raina Wari,
faux flowers festooned her hair.

A Lord of the Skies
broke the sound barrier.
at precisely 1300 hours
stifling calls to *Jumma namaaz*.

Startled,
stray dogs howled
at a gunmetal sky.
Lennon's *Imagine*,

swirling in my head
Loh—le—ta,
in Grandpa's shiny Chevy,
slid from my lap

ending
our
ominous
odyssey.

Rafiq Kathwari

Motherboard

if only i could
redraw her map
revamp her amps
rebuild her microchips
resize her conduits
rift her polarities
ring her circuits
repulse her impulses
raise her thresholds
recess her receptors
rewrite her scripts
retrace her synapses
recall her memories
i would regain Mother

My Mother's Scribe

On Receiving Father at JFK
after His Long Flight
from Kashmir

As I fling my arms wide, he extends a hand.

Rafiq Kathwari

Israeli Patrols Kill 90 Dogs in Arab Town

The New York Times, 14 April 1995

Mother, I'm living in sin with an Egyptian
Jew raised in Paris. We stroll in Central Park
Gaulois, her mutt, off the leash. Lucky he's
not in Hebron, where gods kill dogs for sport.

A Son Writes to His Mother

Mother,
I was the only Muslim in the workshop.
I went on a bit about the Shocking and Awful,
weapons of mass destruction,
Axis of Evil,
mobile chemical lab,
slam dunk,
curve ball,
smoking gun,
mushroom cloud,
cake walk,
liberators,
regime change and
Mission Accomplished.
Civilization's cradle, I said, is a torn country.
I am a witness. I must howl.
In every well in Baghdad
a rafik is weeping while long black coats
(with gas masks)
huddle at the wailing wall
as if prayers could halt smart bombs.
'Rhetoric, not lyric,' my peers echoed Yeats.
'Argue with yourself not others.'
An adjunct shook her head, 'A warhead
soaring from the earth's womb was over the top.
Not *ars poetica*.' Love, your son.

Rafiq Kathwari

Poem without a Title

Your laughter was a car engine
sputtering. Your peers were whiz

kids in the dot com world.
You showed me notes

you'd made in the margins
of all seven volumes by Proust.

You said *Sentimental Education*
wasn't sentimental enough.

You rolled your own leaves reading
Ulysses, finishing it in three nights flat,

but you wished to read it in one day
to parallel the book's action. 'Impossible,'

I said. 'Impossible doesn't exist
in my vocabulary,' you said.

You shook your head at my poem.
'These lines are running all the way to Pakistan.'

I was nearly your dad's age,
yet I looked up to you literally

and physically. My last memory
of you standing against a pine,

at my brother's home with views
of Long Island Sound, aiming

your pee at the tree. You were
the pine you peed on. You were

the sputtering car engine hugging
the tree you peed on moments ago.

I pointed to the crescent moon.
'Wow,' you said, rolling your leaves,

'Let's read *Das Kapital*.'
Nearly 10 years after your childhood

chum, my nephew, was killed
in Afghanistan,

you went from your basement
to *au petit coin retrouvé*,

or depending on mood,
au petit coin perdu—

your Acura parked in a
shuttered garage of your home

Rafiq Kathwari

in Scarsdale.
You reclined on the driver's

seat, popped a pill of Topamax
to dumbfound the snakes

in your mind, chased the pill
with a gulp of Perrier,

and to warm up the car,
you gunned the engine.

For R.Q. 25 December 1972–17 March 2001

After Seeing Caryl Churchill's Seven Jewish Children

A Play for Gaza

Tell her the proper name of things
This is barbed wire
This is a watchtower
These are thermal imaging video cameras
These are 25-foot high concrete slabs
Don't tell her this is a fence
Tell her it's a wall

Teach her to spell a p a r t h e i d

Tell her about nukes in the Negev
Tell her history's most persecuted minority
A specious democracy in the Middle East
Colonial-settler state embracing Biblical pretensions
Is systematically exterminating
The world's most dispossessed tribe

Rafiq Kathwari

Cravings

Will bring you figs in bed
Come to you as clouds
discover the moon
Unstring you knot by knot
Feast with you on the roof
Weave you out of yourself
Uncork your drunkenness
Into cups made from skulls
Wrap you in a robe of words
Chew on your spicy locks
As sometimes in the madhouse
Men gnaw on their chains

Pages from My Father's Diary

Srinagar, Kashmir, Thursday, 14 August 1947

At midnight, Pakistan and Hindustan will be born.
Pakistan Government has instructed
the Superintendent Post Office, Srinagar to fly
Pakistan flag tomorrow on all post office buildings.

Kashmir government doesn't want this to happen.
It's extremely perturbed over it—
feverish political activity in this connection.

It's *Shab-e-Qadar*, an auspicious night,
and tomorrow is *Juma'-atul-widaa*,
when legally two dominions will start to work.

Today, Pakistan Constituent Assembly was addressed
by Lord Mountbatten who, as Governor General,
read the King's message. Then, our most beloved leader,

Qaid-e-Azam Mohammed Ali Jinnah
was sworn in, followed by the First Premier of Pakistan,
Nawabzada Liaquat Ali Khan.

Midnight, sat attentively with friends near the radio
tuning to Lahore. The clock struck 12. Announcer
approached the mike. My heart missed a beat.

Rafiq Kathwari

'Pakistan Broadcasting Service,' he said.
Pakistan has come into existence. Long Live Pakistan!
Long Live Qaid-e-Azam, its architect and founder!

The broadcast started with Koranic recitations.
We couldn't resist tears for so much was the emotion
and so piercing was every word spoken on the radio,

we all actually went into a sort of trance.
Special broadcast ended at 1 A.M.
After that, we talked till 3 A.M.

Srinagar, Kashmir, Friday, 15 August 1947

People were excited early, stringing up
Pakistan flags: White crescent, a star,
white band representing minorities.

Walked to Amira Kadal—holiday today.
The city had a bride's appearance, green, red,
tricolor buntings. Nationalists waved their flag:

Deep red, three white stripes, reflecting Jammu,
Kashmir and Ladakh, a plough in the center
recognizing the tillers. Pakistan flags fluttered

on all post offices, creating great excitement.
People walked for miles to the General Post Office
on the Bund to salute the Pakistan flag.

Drove to Jamia Masjid for *Jummah* in convoy
of cars all displaying Pakistan flags. Huge
congregation. After prayers, drove home.

Was exhausted due to sleeplessness. Rested
until 7 P.M. when two friends picked me up.
We drove to Lake View Hotel for Pakistan Day

party. About 150 gentlemen had responded.
Dinner began and ended with Koranic recitations
under life size statues of Qaid-e-Azam.

Rafiq Kathwari

When I Ask

How does it rain?
You rap a bead of sweat on your forehead

When I ask
How does lightning strike?
You glance at me and lower your eyes

When I ask
How does day meet night?
You veil your face with hair

When I ask
Where does music get its magic?
You lace your talk with honey

When I ask
What good is yearning?
You snuff a candle with your robe's hem

Veracity

Homage to Patrick Kavanagh

'May I borrow your donkey?'
A neighbor asked Kavanagh

Who said, 'I'm very sorry,
I loaned out my donkey yesterday.'

At that moment, the donkey brayed
In the barn. The neighbor, believing

The donkey made Kavanagh a liar,
Asked, 'Then what is that I hear?'

Kavanagh replied, 'Friend, are you going
To believe me or a donkey?'

Rafiq Kathwari

Karl Marx Ignites the Millennials

Ah! Come! How can you not be roused. You are nothing but you are everything. Recharge your iPhones. From each according to his feed to each according to his need. In times of global deceit tweeting the truth puts you in the driver's seat. Highway to hell is paved with fake tweets. Take a knee. Raise a fist. Do it twice: First as history. Then, as tragedy. Rage!

Ask the drones of democracy, Masters of Business Administration, what else is there in their dens of depravity besides electronic hallucinations, market rallies, blow-dried heads squawking, mad money spiritualists, Ponzi pirates, daybreak business briefs, nighttime rundowns, snorting bulls, bashful bears, quarterly yearnings, a spill of crooked graphs? Rage!

Women on the March place a halo back on family values. Disrupt patriarchies that claim your wombs as mere tombs of production. Ban gunrunners who hawk capitalism past its sell-by date. Exorcise temples, churches, and mosques for religion is the pox of the poor hurting for pride. Abolish Wall Street. You have nothing. Unite! Disrupt! Inspire! Reignite! Rage!

Whirling

—Hebrew Home, The Bronx

Mother sobs
in short bursts

I lean over
brush my cheek

against hers
on the pillow

What's wrong?
'Look at Tarek,'

she wails
'he's drowning

For the love of Allah
save my son.

Look my *beta*
he's whirling'

I'm curious
how she knows

Tarek's been swept away
by a rip tide

Rafiq Kathwari

in Goa
the sea yielded

his corpse
a day later

We hid
the news

from Mother—
she'd be beyond grief

for Tarek
youngest of six

even if 62
was her baby

I wonder
voices

she's been hearing
since I was a kid

Is this where poetry
comes from?

A Mother's Eulogy for Her Son

>He
>was strong
>and handsome
>I buried him
>deep in my heart
>and turned
>myself into
>my own grave

Rafiq Kathwari

Mother Writes to Admiral of the Fleet Louis Francis Albert Victor Nicholas Mountbatten, 1st Earl Mountbatten of Burma (born Prince Louis of Battenberg), Last Viceroy of India, Cuckolded by Nehru, Assassinated by the IRA

27 August 2019

Dear Lord Louis,

Last night I dreamt we were flying
on an Oriental rug above graveyards

of the Kashmir valley occupied by India
your hand clasped securely in mine.

We chased our own shadows
over the barbed wire architecture

of the Line of Control
into Pakistan-occupied Kashmir.

'My sixth child was born here, just
years after the Partition,' I said,

but the wind dispersed my words
as we swirled above shiny rivers.

'The Punjab!' you said. 'Land
of five rivers dressed in wheat.

My Mother's Scribe

Here, feudal landlords pressed
Jinnah to demand Partition.'

You steered us through
battalions of monsoon clouds

to the land's edge—Karachi.
'We created Pakistan,' you said,

smirking, 'in order to prevent the
Soviets from using this warm port.'

I was ruffled. 'You're lost in the past.'
I said, 'The past rots the future.'

We soared again above Turkey
'WWI waging down there still,'

you said, laughing. My hair
was tangled. We created waves

in the air. I still had eyes
in my head, a voice in my throat.

I was a tunnel through which light
cascaded into darkness to the edge

of Europe. We slipped below
clouds, hovering above an island.

Rafiq Kathwari

I couldn't remember the last time
I had seen so many shades of green.

I was dumb with happiness.

A postcard-size castle rose up
to greet us. 'I've a leaping impulse,'

you said, unclasped your hand
from mine—a royal crane swooped

down to a boat wreck. Savage waves
broke their bones against jagged rocks.

A splash at the castle's edge.
A lull. Then, the Lion of Kashmir

alit on a rock roared '*Azadi*'
at the foam through which you entered

into the sea. My heart pounded.
I screamed, '*Pani Pani*' rousing

my caregiver, Sabila, dozing
on an Ethan Allen black leather recliner

next to my bed at the Hebrew Home.
The Bronx. Yours, Maryam, Mother of Christ.

My Dinner with Agha Ashraf Ali

You light a candle
carp the darkness

with your usual flourish
debone a carp

add a pinch of salt
in your carpeted kitchen

discourse on the next course
to scrape or not the fish head

gaadkalley honorific
you offer a scrap of history

bestowed once by Kashmiris
on the Big Crap who was fishy

We seize the day
before the diem carpe us

and raise our wineglass
to the disappeared carpenters

of Kashmir
a parched paradise

    In memoriam (18 August 1922 –8 August 2020)

Rafiq Kathwari

The Day I Was My Sister's Chaperone

Tall tan stranger in safari suit
flew from Kenya to Kashmir
to woo her at the Shalimar—

fountain's edge—
she raised the hem
of her sari to her ankles

he rolled the cuffs
of his pants to his knees.
Their toes touched.

She waved—
a gleam on her finger
caught my gaze.

Amorous Lover
amidst lotus buds,
shikarawallahs

sliced
Dal lake
with heart-shaped oars.

For My Nephew Omar on His Engagement to Nadia

This small box conceals
a porcelain elephant,

rigged up howdah,
Kashmir-style sapphire

on forehead—
an inner eye.

Conch shell ears fanning out,
supple trunk cradles

a bird's nest
without breaking the eggs.

'A matriarch of her herd,'
the woman who sold it said.

'175 years old, maybe older.
Japan seal on sole'

Parting with this
I have long held dear —

Rafiq Kathwari

a metaphor
for trials of love

I myself
have yet to endure.

    29 October 2005
    Beaver Dam, Wisconsin

Mother Writes to the Father of her Children,
her Long-Deceased Husband

January 2020

Father of my children, listen, please,
there was commotion yesterday
on our Memory Floor.

My caregiver, Sabila, rushed into my room,
'Ammi' she said, 'someone named Natan
Yahoo is visiting our floor.

He wants to thank Mrs. Siegler for giving
her estate to kibbutz.' 'Who is Natan Yahoo,'
I asked, '*Whatsakibbutz?*'

Mrs. Siegler's a shrunken prune
in Room 217 down the hall.
Sometimes, she stands at my door,

'Kashmir,' she says, 'Kashmir,
is that where wool comes from?'
My door is marked with memories.

Rafiq Kathwari

Father of my children, listen, please,
where're my gloves of gold?
Forgive me for asking.

Father of my children, listen, please,
all I ever wished for was a home
of my own, a tray heaped with fruits

of winter in summer, of summer
in winter. I forgive myself
for wishing this sad splendor.

Father of my children, listen, please,
I forgive you for bringing home
a new wife. Islam permits a husband

to remarry, I told Sabila,
'If he's unhappy with his first wife,
provided she gives him permission,

but father of my children never asked.'
Sabila shook her head, bit her lips.
We hugged. I consoled her.

Father of my children, listen, please,
I've dug deeper into the cold marrow
of my bones, but I can't find

smidgen of forgiveness
for such contempt,
such condescension.

Listen,
Father of my children,
listen, please,

my sigh's restraint is itself a sigh.
Yours, etc. Maryam Jan
Hebrew Home, The Bronx

Rafiq Kathwari

Found in Translation

'Give me hair dye,' Mother says.
Harry the shrink strokes his beard,

'I'm proud of it,' he says.
'Operation Doctor Sahib,'

She points to the mole on her nose.
'God's gift,' he says. She shows him

Her ulna fractured in a recent fall.
'Make it as it was.'

Harry the shrink displays his bruised wrist,
'Fell off the bike when I was young.'

She removes her slip-ons: Girl's feet,
red polish chipped at cuticles.

'Slice off my bunions.'
Harry the shrink removes his socks,

exposing big misshapen toes.
Mother glares at me, reclined

as usual on the couch,
translating Urdu, 'What

does this decrepit man know?
My life is ahead of me.'

My Mother's Scribe

Half-moon above the table
Her face by candlelight

Her upper lip twitches
My right leg flutters

In All Things Be Men
The school motto on my cap

Parker fountain pen
Gold-plated nib

Waterman's ink
Eggshell paper

My blue-black fingers
Pilot her fervent verses

To Prime Ministers of the World
A moth at a candle's edge

Flame flickering
Only calligraphy at her robe's hem

Rafiq Kathwari

Where Are the Snows of Yesteryear?

Mais ou sont les neiges d'antan?

—Villon

It's pretentious to compare this black and white photo
to *The Daughters of Edward Darley Boit*,
Sargent painted in 1882, often paired with *Las Meninas*,
Velasquez painted in 1656. Pretension is underrated.

My love of such paintings compels me to contextualize
this photo taken in Murree, Pakistan, in 1953; six years
after India divided herself.

The matriarch in the center is the prominent figure.
These could just as well be all her children, her brood.
She has a gentle presence, a poignancy about her.

My Mother's Scribe

An older boy, standing straight, his shoulders squared,
smirking, seems unsure about something, but he's facing it,
a white scarf around his neck, a patch of snow on his coat.

He is counterpoint to the man in a trench coat on the right.
They're both in strong positions, but dominated by the matriarch,
her head tilted towards the older boy. This is the first pairing,
left side of the triangle.

Another woman is leaning into the man in the trench coat,
a shawl loosely draped around her. She is aligned not with
the matriarch, but with the man in the trench coat.
Are they a couple? Are the two boys their children?
This is the second pairing. The right side of the triangle.

A young boy looks puzzled. Standing between the matriarch,
the woman with shawl draped around her, and the man
in the trench coat. It's a child's fear, unsure of what's going on.
Yet, even though he looks puzzled, he's safe at base of the triangle.

Nobody is smiling here (except for the smirk on older boy's face).
Everybody looks serious, perhaps they think they need to.
There is a lot of fresh snow, drifting up tree trunks, limbs
naked in the background, revealing a grand architecture.

We're in deep winter. Nobody is dressed for deep winter;
even the shawl matriarch has loosely draped around her
is too thin. All have been summoned here hastily perhaps,

away from a glowing fire; they've been asked to run

outside, pose for the photo, wait for the photographer
to click so that they can all be free to run inside
and get warm again.

Or, perhaps there is no photographer.
The man in the trench coat sitting upright on packed snow
has screwed on a tripod his Agfa Rolleiflex.
All are intently watching the timer, sound of the shutter,
(remember, it's 1953), the lens closing, freeing everybody.

Is the matriarch at the triangle's apex a mother-in-law,
or a mother? What gives her poignancy? Are some children
missing? Why does her face convey loss? It's not a power
expression, but the look of a woman who has had her hopes

and those of her children dashed. It wouldn't matter if the two
boys were not hers. She would still be a moving spirit
and her poignancy would embrace those who were not there,
forming a set of relationships. I am the little boy standing

in front of my mother, my head no higher than her belly.
There is a dusting of snow on my oversized coat, a hand-me-
down heirloom. I am five, wide-eyed, fearful yet sheltered—
seeing my future 66 years thence in another continent.

OBIT

Mother passed away in her sleep at the Hebrew Home in the Bronx. I visited her last on 7 March 2020. The Hebrew Home locked down on the 10th due to the Covid-19 pandemic. Mother died alone on 31st March. She was 96.

Mother's caregiver, Sabila from Kathmandu, who, over the last 10 years, created an extraordinary bond with Mother—called her Ammi Jan — once gave Mother a framed picture of Mother India or *Bharat Mata*. Mother reciprocated by teaching Sabila the first surah of the Koran which Sabila recited most delightfully and by heart: *Iyyaka Na Budu Wa Iyyaka Nastaaeen.*

So, here's how Sabila saw my mother wrapped in a bright sari, superimposed on a map of India painted on a box of safety matches. It's incendiary.

Kashmir crowns the Mata who wields Shiva's powerful trident in her right hand. A multi-color flag erases Afghanistan and Pakistan. Left-hand shadows Bangladesh gesturing towards Myanmar. Her foot seems bigger than pearl-shaped Sri Lanka which forms the central story of the Hindu epic Ramayana.

Here's how Mother told the story, choosing the folkloric Kashmiri term, *Dapaan*—they say—to start her tale.

Dapaan, Rama saw Sita bathing nude in Sitaharan, a spring near the Line of Control in Kashmir. It was lust at first sight. *Dapaan*, the demon king Ravana abducted Sita to Sri Lanka to avenge a previous wrong. Rama flew in anger south to Sri Lanka in his glitzy winged chariot. *Dapaan*, the chariot was Made in Prehistoric India, using indigenous materials. *Dapaan*, Hanuman, the son of Vayu, god of the wind, steered the chariot. *Dapaan*, clouds cloaked the chariot to foil discovery by enemy radar. *Dapaan*, Rama shot a divine arrow which pierced Ravana in the heart and killed him. *Dapaan*, Rama flew Sita back to Sitaharan where they lived happily until India partitioned herself, tearing apart 15 million souls, the largest migration of people in modern history.

Dapaan, Hindutva has been weaponized to impose mythology upon history to create Greater India—*Akhand Baharat*, united and undivided Hindu *Rashtra* from Afghanistan to Myanmar. *Dapaan*, Kashmir strikes at the heart of this nirvana because of its Muslim majority.

Dapaan, every summer the army shields thousands of Hindu pilgrims who spread the legs of a virgin glacier in Kashmir to worship Shiva's icy lingam thawing in a cave—daring an ecological disaster. *Dapaan*, Hindutva is a pandemic.

Dapaan, Neanderthals of Nagpur are marching into Kashmir to the drumbeat of Hindutva supremythology: *Gharwapsi, zaminjihad, lovejihad* to herald *acche din*. *Dapaan*, fascists clasp opposite concepts to serve their own puffery. *Dapaan*, Kashmiris will be told to hold the scalpel for their own execution to chill the blood of Neanderthals.

Dapaan, prepare for the moment when history throws up a rainbow over the Zabarvan. Rainbows are ephemeral. Preparedness is everything. When they ask, *Azadi ka matlab kya*? Shout out loud—*Jamhooriya, Jamhooriya*. *Dapaan*, poets will be caged because poetry is the fuel of Azadi.

Mother was born in Abiguzar, Srinagar. She is buried in Putnam County, NY in a universalist cemetery politely renamed Memorial Garden, where people of diverse faiths are dying to get in.

R.I.P Maryam Jan, Mother of Christ. 5 March 1924–31 March 2020.

GLOSSARY

GOD IN TAILCOATS MAKES A HOUSE CALL

- Inspired by 'The Hanging Man' by Sylvia Plath.

MOTHER WRITES TO PRESIDENT EISENHOWER

- Mother dictated her letters in Kashmiri, her mother tongue, or sometimes in Urdu. The author, as his mother's scribe, translated those letters into English, his adopted language. All other work presented here is in English unless stated otherwise.

SUNDAY BATH IN THE CUBE

- In the 16th tercet, '...runs down / without touching the handrail,' imagery inspired by Anna Akhmatova 1889–1966.
- Ceasefire Line or Cease Fire Line, now called The Line of Control, divides Kashmir into two parts: India-controlled, and Pakistan-controlled Kashmir. Pakistan calls its part of Kashmir, *Azad* or Free. Pakistani politicians say, 'Kashmir is Pakistan's jugular vein.' Indian politicians say, 'Kashmir is an integral part of India.'

WHAT HAPPENED TO A WORLD

- K2: Second highest peak in the world, some say it is even higher than the Mt. Everest.

- *Eid al-Adha*: One of Islam's most sacred days. To establish centrality for Ishmael (Father of the Arab Nation) Muslims say it was he—not Isaac—God commanded Abraham to sacrifice. The day is marked by festivity and sacrifice of goats and lambs.
- *Bismillah*: In the name of Allah.

MOTHER WRITES TO THE TURKISH AMBASSADOR IN KARACHI

- In stanza three, imagery inspired after reading *Concerto al-Quds* by Adonis, translated from the Arabic by Khaled Mattawa (Yale University Press, 2017).

I GO BACK TO JUNE 1939 WHEN MY PARENTS WED

- Poem inspired by 'I Go Back to May 1973' by Sharon Olds.

MOTHER WRITES TO INDIRA GANDHI

- Indira Ji: Sounds like Madam G, a form of respect for Mrs. Indira Gandhi (1917–1984), former Prime Minister of India, the only woman prime minister of India to date.
- Emergency: In India, 'the Emergency' refers to a 21-month period in 1975–77 when Indira Gandhi unilaterally had a state of emergency declared across the country, suspending fundamental human rights guaranteed under India's constitution.
- Brahmachari: Reportedly, during the Emergency, Mrs. Gandhi was having an affair with Dhirendra Brahmachari, her yoga teacher.
- Shor: Noise
- Shanti: Peace/ solitude

INDIRA GANDHI RESPONDS

- No relation to Mahatma Gandhi. Indira was the daughter of Jawaharlal Nehru, India's first Prime Minister. She married Feroze Gandhi (no relation to the Mahatma). Hence, the last name.

OLD FORMS WILL NOT BE ENTERTAINED

- Alternative gods: David Barsamian (born 1945) is an Armenian-American radio broadcaster, writer, and the founder and director of Alternative Radio, a Boulder-Colorado based weekly public affairs program heard over 250 radio stations worldwide. David has had a long love affair with India where his guru taught him how to play the sitar. On his radio show, David once aired his thoughts about his recent visit to Kashmir to his listeners. The regime in India was listening as well and subsequently, in 2011, when David landed at New Delhi airport, he was deported.

HALLUCINATIONS

- Shalimar: Famous Mughal garden in Srinagar, the summer capital of Kashmir.

MOTHER LEANS AGAINST THE ISLAND

- Lazy Susan is a rotating tray to ease the sharing of food around the table.

MOTHER HAS THE LAST WORD

- Imagery in 7th and 8th tercets inspired by 'The Eskimo's Twelve Expressions of White,' James Ragan, *Lusions* (Grove, 1997).

- Ativan and Zyprexa: Anti-anxiety and anti-psychotic drugs respectively.

I TRANSLATE MOTHER'S DREAM FOR HARRY THE SHRINK

- Champion Lovemaker: In Sufism this is an endearing term for the Prophet Mohammed, PBUH.

DR. QURESHI DARES MY MOTHER

- Jan: My life; a term of endearment.
- Ammi: Mother
- Betas: It means sons, also a term of endearment.
- Mashallah: Praise Allah.
- Brown Buddha: Big night out.

I HALLUCINATE A BOMB BLAST IN BAGGAGE CLAIM

- Dupatta: A veil or a scarf.
- Mohammedan angels: From 'Howl' by Allen Ginsberg, *Howl and other Poems* (City Lights, 1956).
- Kush: A strain of Cannabis Indica.

KISMET

- 'I grit my teeth, glaring / at a fantasy Orient, thinking / of Iraq in ruins today…'
- I wrote this poem post 'Shock and Awe'.
- Fantasy Orient: Colonizers recreated in their home cities a fantastic idea of the Orient to show the glories of empire to their own people. The notion was dissected eloquently, plumbing the arts and literature of the 18th and 19th centuries, by the unrivaled Edward Said in his powerful work, *Culture and Imperialism* (Chatto & Windus,1993).

LAST NIGHT I DREAMT I WAS IN KASHMIR AGAIN

- Chinar: Kashmir's plane tree; Chi means What; Nar: Fire. What Fire!
- Kangri: A hand-held clay pot enclosed in a bright wicker basket. The embers of autumn leaves are stoked in the pot to keep hands and feet warm during Kashmir's harsh winter.
- Pheran: A loose mantel worn by both women and men, especially during winter.
- Shikara: A bit wider than a Venetian gondola, with cushioned seats embellished with Suzani style or crewel embroidery.
- Overall imagery in this poem influenced by the works of Agha Shahid Ali.

DRIVING LOLITA IN THE WORLD'S MOST MILITARIZED ZONE

- Zero Bridge: Historically, nine bridges span the Jhelum in Srinagar. In the '60s when a new bridge was located before the First Bridge it was named Zero Bridge in order not to disrupt the historical sequence, from one to nine. Now, new bridges are named after politicians.
- Half-Widows: Women who do not know whether or not their husbands whom the military has disappeared are dead or alive.
- *Yehthe laege nave tav taylephone*: Install a telephone here.
- Nightingales sang of joy, not sorrow. Keats said the nightingale does not sing of sorrow and if you think it does, it sings of the joy of sorrow or, to paraphrase Brecht, 'there will be singing and dancing in dark times about the dark times'.

A SON WRITES TO HIS MOTHER

- *Rafik* means a friend in Arabic and 'a companion of the journey' in Farsi.

AFTER SEEING CARYL CHURCHILL'S SEVEN JEWISH CHILDREN—A PLAY FOR GAZA

- A major playwright in the tradition of Bertolt Brecht and Samuel Beckett, Caryl Churchill has won several awards. The play was penned and staged in response to Israel's most recent brutal massacre in Gaza. 'Operation Cast Lead,' Israel's carefully calculated and long-planned 22-day December 2008–January 2009 attack on Gaza, resulted in the deaths of 1,300 Gazans, the majority unarmed civilians, and left communities in shambles.

CRAVINGS

- After Jalāl ad-Dīn Muhammad Rūmī (1207–1273).

PAGES FROM MY FATHER'S DIARY

- My father started writing a journal in English, from 1934, when he started his law studies at Aligarh Muslim University, to 1999 when he died. It's one man's eyewitness account of history. I have a closet full of his journals which I hope to share with the world before I too am called back.
- Mohammed Ali Jinnah 25 December1876–11 September 1948: Jinnah served as the leader of the All-India Muslim League from 1913 until Pakistan's creation on 14 August 1947,

and then as Pakistan's first Governor-General until his death. He is revered in Pakistan as Quaid-i-Azam (Great Leader) and Baba-i-Qaum (Father of the Nation).
- *Shab-e-Qadar* also known as Laylat al-Qadr, Night of Decree, Night of Measures, is an Islamic observance that marks the anniversary of the night Prophet Mohammad (PBUH) received the first verses of the Koran (Qu'ran). Many Muslims devote their time to reading the Koran during this period.
- *Juma'-atul-widaa*: Friday of farewell, also called al-Jumu'ah al-Yateemahor, the orphaned Friday, is the last Friday in the month of Ramzan before *Eid-ul-Fitr*.

WHEN I ASK

For Annie Zaidi

- A lovely or a lousy (depending on one's taste) translation of few verses from a qawwali sung by the late great Ustad Nusrat Fateh Ali Khan.

VERACITY

- After Mullah Nasreddin Hooja, the 13th century satirist who lived in present-day Turkey.

KARL MARX IGNITES THE MILLENNIALS

- The second stanza is a loaded recreation of a short poem about Karl Marx by the poet-philosopher Muhammed Iqbal (1877–1938).

MOTHER WRITES TO ADMIRAL OF THE FLEET LOUIS FRANCIS ALBERT VICTOR NICHOLAS MOUNTBATTEN...

- *Pani Pani:* Water Water

MY DINNER WITH AGHA ASHRAF ALI

In fond memory of Agha Shahid Ali (February 1949–December 2001)

- *Gaadkalley*: Head of a fish in Kashmiri. The reference is to Sheikh Mohammed Abdullah, 1905–1982, one of the most important political figures in the modern history of Kashmir who was endowed with a big head or, metaphorically, his head was in the clouds.
- Pandit Nehru, India's First Prime Minister and father of Indira Gandhi, jailed Sheikh Abdullah for several years because he decreed that those who till the land in Kashmir own it. Consequently, he abolished a century of serfdom in Kashmir instituted by the Dogra dynasty. The Sheikh earned the title, 'Lion of Kashmir'.

THE DAY I WAS MY SISTER'S CHAPERONE

- Shalimar: In Sanskrit means 'abode of love'. It is a terraced garden with fountains built in 1619 on the banks of Dal Lake by the Mughal Emperor, Jahangir, to please his wife, Noor Jahan.
- *Shikarawallahs*: Like the Venetian gondoliers, the *shikarawallahs* ply boats, their shikaras are wider than the gondolas. See the note under 'Last Night I Dreamt I Was in Kashmir Again'.
- Amorous Lover: Name aboard on a shikara.

MOTHER WRITES TO THE FATHER OF HER CHILDREN, HER LONG-DECEASED HUSBAND

- 'Gloves of gold': Inspired by 'The People', a poem by Pablo Neruda.
- 'Fruits / of winter in summer, / of summer in winter': Inspired by 'The Sky on Earth', a poem by Adonis, translated from the Arabic by Khaled Mattawa.

WHERE ARE THE SNOWS OF YESTERYEAR?

For Suzanne Morriss-Batchelder whose critique of the photo made the poem.

- Many thanks to Gabriel Rosenstock who suggested the title and chose the music that ends the narration in the video version of this poem uploaded to YouTube.

OBIT

- *Iyyaka Na Budu Wa Iyyaka Nastaaeen:* You (alone) we worship; You (alone) we ask for help.
- *Gharwapsi*: Return home—(to Kashmir of Hindu myths).
- *Zaminjihad*: The East India Company sold Kashmir to the Rajput Dogras who enslaved Kashmiris for over 100 years. Sheikh Abdullah, with a swirl of his fountain pen, deemed tillers the owners of land they till, freed Kashmiris from serfdom, made peasants landowners—*zamindar*s and earned the honorific, 'Lion of Kashmir'. This scared India's suave socialist prime minister, Pandit Nehru, and his inner circle of prominent and privileged Kashmiri pandits. They exiled Sheikh Abdullah for nearly 20 years.

- *Lovejihad*: Hindutva drive to wage war at love between young Muslims and Hindus.
- *Acche din*: Good days
- *Azadi ka matlab kya?*: What does liberty mean?
- *Jamhooriya, Jamhooriya:* Democracy, Democracy.
- The illustration of *Bharat Mata* is attributed to Masood Hussain.

GRATITUDE/*SHUKRIYA*

'You're not my son, if you don't join the family business.' I thank my deceased dad for airing his aspirations for me. Many fathers I know want the best for their children as it's they who see what is best for them. Aha! There's the rub.

My political views were shaped by a remarkable film, *The Battle of Algiers*, directed by Gillo Pontecorvo (1919–2006), that I first saw in 1967, when I was 19, at the Palladium, Srinagar's Cinema Paradiso which was subsequently demolished—an army bunker now marks the memory. The film taught me an enduring lesson that the Three-Year Degree Course (TDC) at the Sri Pratap College couldn't. The film contextualized history for me: We are not alone. There are concurrent historical battles being waged beyond Kashmir. Women are heroines in the struggle, not reduced to merely weeping. United, men and women of the Kasbah, using all means necessary, drove out the French who rolled up their Algerian Domicile Certificates they had awarded themselves during 132 years of occupation. *The Battle of Algiers* grounded me forever on the side of the oppressed, the side of *Azadi*.

Here in New York, for many years I searched dreadfully for a father figure, often transferring my need onto Harry the Shrink whom I met twice weekly for over a decade. He was a Freudian who waited for me to make my own discoveries over time, but I was in a hurry. I took no joy in slipping him three $100 bills under the table every week, the going rate in the '80s. Had Harry the Shrink been a disciple of Jung, had he lit a fire under my bony ass, perhaps my dread would have eased. Now, years later, having made a few discoveries, I'm grateful to Harry the Shrink for rewiring my inner machinery which has enabled me to dig deeper for more than gold.

An omniscient Divinity who I believe hovers above me like a hummingbird, guided me to Nathan Ancell, or him to me. The founder of Ethan Allen Interiors, a home décor company, where I worked for nearly 20 years managing a handful of affiliated organizations; Ancell, a Moses sans beard, but with a prosperous belly, embraced me. 'There are four questions you must ask of yourself,' he said, 'who are you, why are you here, where are you going and why aren't you already there?' Ancell gave me the keys to begin to unlock the answers—keys, I later discovered, could well have been cut by Proust who devised a questionnaire and provided keys in his *Les confidences de salon* (Drawing room confessions).

Nat Ancell also gave me his season tickets to the Met Opera where, after seeing Wagner's Ring Cycle, I began to see myself as Siegfried in a cave, smelting iron to forge my sword with which I would fearlessly slay a dragon, climb a mountain to claim my prize, my Brünnhilde. Life rarely imitates art, yet the joy at the Met was a given. Nat, R.I.P: Return if Possible.

Thank you Leah Solomon for introducing me in the late '80s to the formidable Susan Shapiro who every Tuesday evening for over 30 years in good faith and enlightened self-interest had opened the door of her West village apartment where a group of established writers steered wannabes like myself who came in often with a two-page poem and went out with a one liner, our best babies lay murdered on the parquet floor. For instance see poem on page 57, that years ago was pared down to the bone, but now speaks to our social distancing requirements under a pandemic.

My Mother's Scribe

The immortal Kashmiri-American poet, Agha Shahid Ali, who chiseled a fine name for himself in the small incestuous circle of contemporary American poets, and whom I had known growing up in Kashmir (we were neighbors), urged me to write about my mother's mental challenges which both Shahid and I agreed is a compelling subject. This collection is as much a homage to my mother as it is to three near and dear departed souls: Shahid, Aslum and Tariq, the latter two my oldest and youngest brothers respectively.

As Shahid would have said, for the usual and unusual reasons, heartfelt gratitude, first of all, to my mother's caregivers for over two decades in New York: Babita, Davinder, Donna, Giselle, Sabila, Shami, Shanta and Yeshi, all did what they do best, many did so under the loving direction of Dr. Mag Bag on the Memory Floor at the Hebrew Home, a blessed place for the aged, in The Bronx.

Next, gratitude for my peers at the writing workshop (an offshoot of Susan's) on the Upper West Side: Barbara, Bob, Gerry, Harold, Jeffrey, Kayla, Patrick, Rob, Steven and Yvonne.

I'm grateful also to more peers, you know who you are, at the Friday Evening Poetry Gathering at the Symposium on West 113th Street, where we parse the ghazals of Ghalib under the watchful gaze of Professor Emeritus, Frances Pritchett, and where a pitcher of Limniona helps bear the ephemeral glance of Ghalib's beloved muse.

A roomful of extraordinary souls whose friendship has sustained me during the pandemic as well as esoteric times deserve my gratitude: Saima Afreen, John Van de Brooke, Adger Cowans, Tabish Din, Lisa Frank and John Walsh (Doire Press), Brian Drolet, the Dowlings, the Erminis, Alicia Faugier, Elena and Andrea Gelcich, Barbara Grill, Kabita Das Gupta, the Haiders, Chennel Hosein, Sally

Ann Jacobs, Gabriela Jurosz-Landa, the Levys, Brian Lynch, Joyce Maio, Shura McCletchie, Jose Medina, Rosenda and Salman Meer, Melissa Nolan, Cathal Quinn, Waseem and Basharat Rasool, the Rosenstocks, Antonio, Sarah and Samuel Schneider, John Seth, the Shahdads, Shirley Cherin Sigler (100! Wow! And counting), Priya Singh and, the best for the last, offsprings of Shabia and 'Chotu': Zainab, Zain and Zahra.

Kashmiri stories matter. I'm raining gratitude on those colleagues I know personally who are telling stories about Kashmir in Kashmiri, Hinglish, Irish and English, exhausting the Fine Arts: Poetry, painting, photography, film, writing novels and memoirs, plumbing anthropology, law and history, heartily singing and dancing in dark times about the dark times: Sameetah Agha, Tariq Ali, Dibyesh Anand, Aditi Angiras, David Barsamian, Farah Bashir, Shahnaz Bashir, Suzanne Morriss-Batchelder, Angana Chatterji, Oniza Drabu, Haley Duschinski, Azad Essa, Uzma Falak, Sabbah Haji, Justine Hardy, Masood Hussain, Muzamil Jaleel, Yusuf Jameel, Mohamad Junaid, Sanjay Kak, Hafsa Kanjwal, Nitasha Kaul, Akhil Katyal, Fawzia Afzal Khan, Heena Khan, George Mathew, Aliya Nazki, Tahira Naqvi, Khurram Pervez, Basharat Peer, Mridu Rai, Gabriel Rosenstock, Arundhati Roy, Raza Rumi, Malik Sajad, Beena Sarwar, Fahad Shah, Niya Shahdad, Suchitra Vijayan, Mirza Waheed, Andrew Whitehead, Asiya Zahoor and Ather Zia.

For the unusual reasons, I am grateful to the fearless Arpita Das, my publisher, who said, 'Yes, why not,' when I asked if she'd be interested in reading my manuscript for possible publication; Tanya Singh at Yoda Press who slayed the copyediting beast over and over again; Saira Wasim, an artist extraordinaire who agreed to do the striking cover for this book despite home-schooling her children during pandemic times; Aisha Mastoor, legendary poet writing in Kashmiri, who translated my dedication; Abbas and Azra Raza, good friends and editors at 3quardsdaily dot com, a precious literary blog, where I rage every third Monday and where many of these poems were first published individually. I'm grateful to Margaret Dimond, publicist, who gave me the social-media makeover that says, dark, handsome, creative! Folks, Perception is Reality.

What, then, is Reality? A generous gift from my brother Farooq, and sister-in law Farida enabled me to complete this manuscript and an additional one as well, *Versions: Selected Poems of Iqbal* translated from the Urdu into English, particularly for a 21st century audience.

With his usual grace and wit, Farooq financed our mother's reinvention, enabling the family to give Mother a substantial measure of dignity in the last 20 years of her life in New York that she had been substantially denied in the previous 76 in Kashmir.

Thank you, Uncle Amin for your timely financial support during difficult times after Tariq's death in Goa and subsequent burial in Srinagar. You know that I have a good track record in returning a loan, even if it is from a rich uncle and even if it is a lousy two lakh rupees.

In our own way, best we know how, sisters Aisha in Srinagar, Mahmuda in Nairobi, cousins Suraya in Toledo and Sarvat in Delhi and my niece Misbah in Cairo and nephew Asif in Cleveland—we all ring one another often, but my other five nieces, one nephew, grand nephews and nieces—do only rarely. O, well, all happy relatives are alike; each unhappy relative is unhappy ... Enough, open up your laptops, folks. Let's win the Battle of Kashmir.

August 2020
New York, NY

FIRST PUBLICATION CREDITS

Grateful acknowledgment is made to the editors of the following publications where these poems, some of which have been subsequently substantially revised, originally appeared:

Traditional Media

'Sunday Bath (in the Cube)' was anthologized in *'With Our Eyes Wide Open': Poems of the New American Century*, Editor, Douglas Valentine, West End Press, 2014.

'Jewel House Ghazal' anthologized previously as 'In Another Country' in *Ravishing Disunities: Real Ghazals in English*, Editors, Agha Shahid Ali and Sarah Suleri Goodyear, Wesleyan Poetry Series, 2000.

'Birds of Paradise' was previously published in a different form as 'My Pious Grandfather,' in *Quarto*, Vol. 32, Columbia University, 1996.

'What Happened to a World,' was previously published in a different form as 'I Remember' in *Quarto*, Vol. 32, Columbia University, 1996.

'Mother Writes to Indira Gandhi' was published as prose, 'Mother's Last Letter,' in *The Observer*, winter issue, Columbia University, 1996–97.

'Hallucinations' was performed on stage by the Columbia University Dramatic Club in fall of 1999.

An earlier version of 'Last Night I Dreamt I was in Kashmir Again' was published as 'Fire Tree' in *Tin House Magazine*, Vol. 3(3), Spring 2002.

Web— Partial List

Many poems here have been published over the past several years on the web, mainly at the literary blog https://www.3quarksdaily.com/3quarksdaily/author/rafiqkathwari where I am a longstanding Monday columnist.

'Capitals: Game Farouk Plays To Keep Mother's Mind Active' was published in *Palestine Chronicle*. Available at https://www.palestinechronicle.com/capitals-game-farouk-plays-to-keep-mothers-mind-active-a-poem, last accessed 3 July 2020.

'God in Tailcoats Makes a House Call' was published as 'Shock and Stoicism' in *Poems from the Beloved*. Available at
https://poemsfromthebeloved.tumblr.com/post/73296162874/shock-and-stoicism-a-doctor-in-tailcoats, last accessed 3 July 2020.

'Mother Writes to her Husband's New Wife' was published as 'To her Husband's New Wife' in *Poems from the Beloved*. Available at https://poemsfromthebeloved.tumblr.com/post/73368593543/mothers-scribe-to-her-husbands-new-wife-i-rule, last accessed 3 July 2020.

'Hallucinations' was published in *Poems from the Beloved*. Available at https://poemsfromthebeloved.tumblr.com/post/73399083102/hallucinations-for-richard-howard-the-servants, last accessed 3 July 2020.

'My Mother's Scribe' was published in *Poems from the Beloved*. Available at https://poemsfromthebeloved.tumblr.com/post/73471947783/my-mothers-scribe-half-moon-above-the-table-her, last accessed 3 July 2020.

'Israeli Patrol Kill 90 Dogs in Arab Town' was published in *Poems from the Beloved*. Available at https://poemsfromthebeloved.tumblr.com/post/73573521918/israeli-patrols-kill-90-dogs-in-arab-town, last accessed 3 July 2020.

Awards and Grants

A portion of this manuscript received the Patrick Kavanagh Award in 2013 from the Patrick Kavanagh Centre in Ireland and, with the assistance of The Irish Arts Council /*An Chomhairle Ealaíon*, was subsequently published in a substantially different form in a limited edition of 300 by Doire Press, Galway, under the name of *In Another Country* (2015). All rights have reverted to the author.

ABOUT THE POET

Rafiq Kathwari, the first Kashmiri recipient of the Patrick Kavanagh Award, obtained an MFA in Creative Writing at Columbia University and an MA in Political and Social Science from the New School University. Rafiq divides his time between New York City, Dublin and Kashmir.

Praise for *In Another Country*

'Rafiq Kathwari is several poets rolled into one, reminding us, by turns, of Ginsberg, Plath and Richard Howard. This diverse collection of poems is autobiographical without being suburban, a window onto domestic experience in post-Partition Kashmir. Also, a reminder that the family romance is always only a step away from civil war.'

—Alfred Corn, author of *Unions* (2000)

'Keenly observed, Kathwari's subjects are the great subjects: family, war, history and love. Whether writing of his "off kilter" mother or harking back to the "speak memory" of his Kashmir childhood forever split by the Partition of 1947, Kathwari writes poetry of brilliant intensity. This is an original and sometimes heart-breaking book and deserves high praise.'

—Colette Inez, author of *The Luba Poems* (2015)

'Rafiq Kathwari's poetry—often set in Kashmir—is breathtakingly beautiful, piercingly honest, wildly exotic yet universal too, as if you put Derek Walcott, Salman Rushdie and Jhumpa Lahiri in a blender.'

—Susan Shapiro, author of *What's Never Said* (2015)

'Vivid, fearless vignettes of the displaced denizens of our global village, poems and prose poems that encompass a myriad of moods and situations, humour and horror, tradition jostling with modernity, autobiographical and family sketches with an aura of magic realism and sheer cussedness about them. *In Another Country* is a bloody marvel!'

—Gabriel Rosenstock, author of *The Naked Octopus* (2013)